Confucius and His Teachings about Life

Children's Ancient History Books

BABY PROFESSOR

EDUCATION KIDS

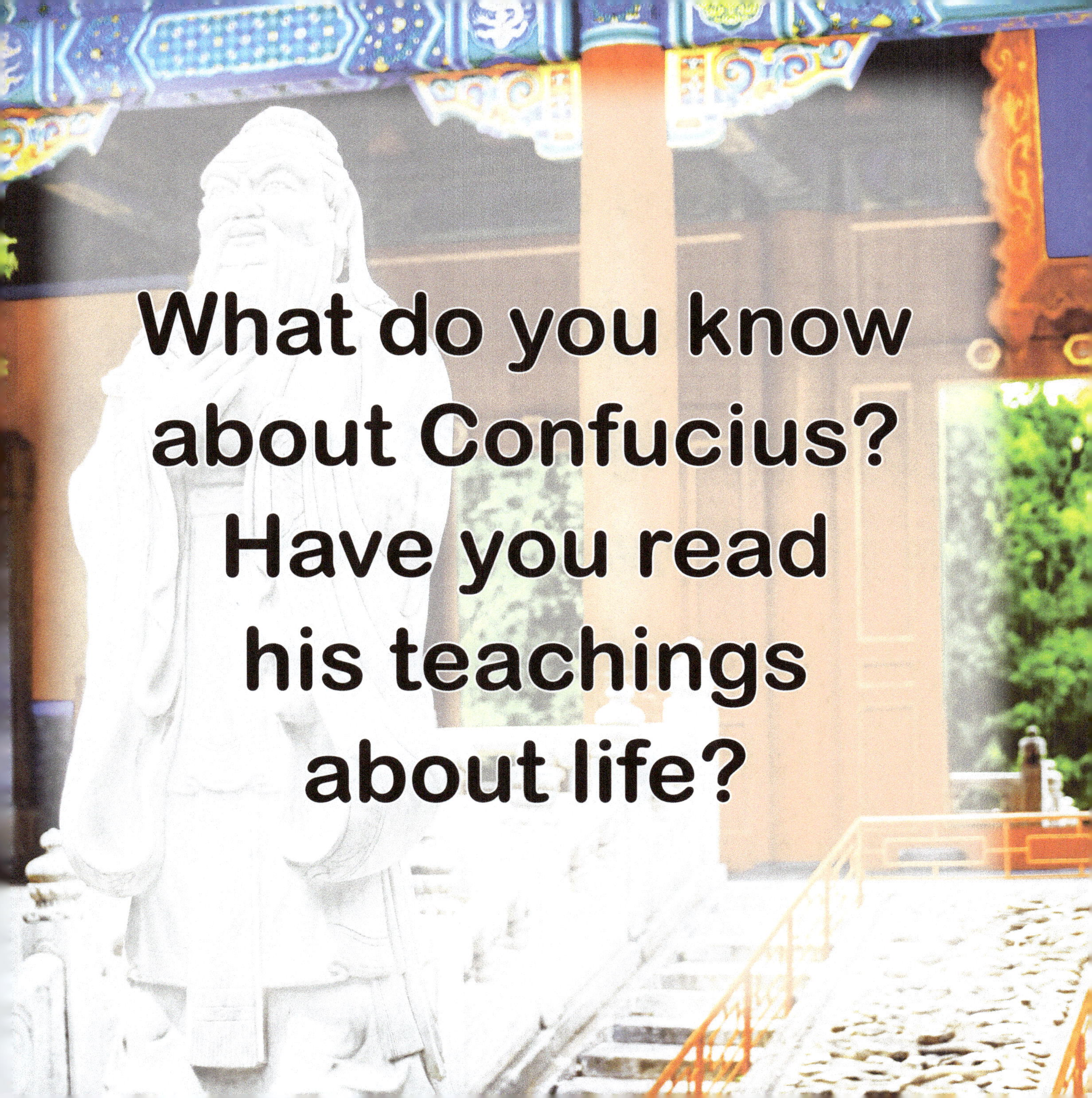
What do you know
about Confucius?
Have you read
his teachings
about life?

In this book you
will learn about the
life and inspiring
teachings of the
most famous man
in Chinese history.

Read on and get to know this great man who has shaped world history.

大成殿

Who was Confucius?

In Chinese, Confucius was known as Kung Fu-tzu. He was born in the state of Lu, in northeast China, in 551 BCE. He father, a military officer, died when Confucius was three years old.

Confucius became as famous as Alexander the Great, Ramses II and other great leaders and emperors in history. However, his greatness was not because he led an army and won in battle. He never ruled a state. Yet, Confucius' great wisdom was heard all over the world and has shaped the soul of China.

Confucius grew up as a poor boy. Nonetheless, he attained a good education. He got married at an early age and became a laborer. He experienced working as a shepherd, clerk, cowherd, and bookkeeper in order to support his family. In 527 BCE Confucius started his new career. He was 24 years old when he started teaching.

As a teacher, he shared with his students the ideas of ancient Chinese wise men. His purpose was to achieve reform in the government, which he condemned as lawless and corrupt.

He became a judge at the age of 50 in 501 BCE. He was in charge of law and order in the state of Lu. Confucius created laws which were based on his personal teachings. Indeed, he was so successful as a judge and lawmaker that crime almost disappeared.

成
殿

Students of Confucius wrote down his teachings, which were compiled in the Sishu, or Four Books. Chinese people have been studying the books for over two thousand years. His followers founded Confucianism.

Confucianism is one of the largest and oldest religions in China, and in the whole world.

Confucius did not make any discovery in science, neither did he make wonderful inventions. But he was looked up to by people all over the world because of his teachings. They definitely showed his great wisdom. His teachings remain as sources of inspiration today.

All people appreciate his Golden Rule, "What you do not wish for yourself, do not do to others" (Analects 12.2). This made him well remembered. This is indeed very inspiring and moves people to always do well. In this way, Confucius taught people to develop compassion for one another. People should treat others the way they wish to be treated.

Confucius gave
importance
to education
as a means of
achieving proper
conduct both
within society and
in government.
For him, the key
to self mastery
is through study
and scholarship.

He clearly emphasized that people must be good. Respecting and honoring their parents and ancestors should be of the utmost importance.

Confucius further encouraged people to practice honesty, and taught that they should be polite and wise. He also inspired leaders to become models of good behavior.

People should
be conscious
of their manner
and speech.
Hence, people
should avoid self-
aggrandizement
or too much
selfishness.
According to
Confucius, people
should be selfless
and practice
self restraint.

Confucius taught
his students
that everything
in life should be
done humbly
and for the good
of others.

Confucius was indeed a great man of wisdom. Ancient China was lucky to have him as a teacher. His strict ideas of how people should behave had an impact that was felt all over the world.

Visit
BABY PROFESSOR
EDUCATION KIDS
www.BabyProfessorBooks.com
to download Free Baby Professor eBooks
and view our catalog of new and exciting
Children's Books